Monthly Profit Tracker

Month	Total Spend	Total Sales	Total Profit

Purchase & Sales Tracker

DATES FROM _____

Item	Purchase Date	Sale Date	Sale Website	Purchase Price	Sale Price	Profit

Total | | | |

Purchase & Sales Tracker

DATES FROM _____

Item	Purchase Date	Sale Date	Sale Website	Purchase Price	Sale Price	Profit

Total

Purchase & Sales Tracker

DATES FROM _____

Item	Purchase Date	Sale Date	Sale Website	Purchase Price	Sale Price	Profit

Total

Purchase & Sales Tracker

DATES FROM _____

Item	Purchase Date	Sale Date	Sale Website	Purchase Price	Sale Price	Profit

Total

Purchase & Sales Tracker

DATES FROM _____

Item	Purchase Date	Sale Date	Sale Website	Purchase Price	Sale Price	Profit

Total | | |

Purchase & Sales Tracker

DATES FROM _____

Item	Purchase Date	Sale Date	Sale Website	Purchase Price	Sale Price	Profit

Total

Purchase & Sales Tracker

DATES FROM _____

Item	Purchase Date	Sale Date	Sale Website	Purchase Price	Sale Price	Profit

Total | | | |

Purchase & Sales Tracker

DATES FROM _____

Item	Purchase Date	Sale Date	Sale Website	Purchase Price	Sale Price	Profit

Total

Purchase & Sales Tracker

DATES FROM _____

Item	Purchase Date	Sale Date	Sale Website	Purchase Price	Sale Price	Profit

Total

Purchase & Sales Tracker

DATES FROM _____

Item	Purchase Date	Sale Date	Sale Website	Purchase Price	Sale Price	Profit

Total

Purchase & Sales Tracker

DATES FROM _____

Item	Purchase Date	Sale Date	Sale Website	Purchase Price	Sale Price	Profit

Total

Purchase & Sales Tracker

DATES FROM _____

Item	Purchase Date	Sale Date	Sale Website	Purchase Price	Sale Price	Profit

Total

Purchase & Sales Tracker

DATES FROM _____

Item	Purchase Date	Sale Date	Sale Website	Purchase Price	Sale Price	Profit

Total

Purchase & Sales Tracker

DATES FROM _____

Item	Purchase Date	Sale Date	Sale Website	Purchase Price	Sale Price	Profit

Total

Purchase & Sales Tracker

DATES FROM _____

Item	Purchase Date	Sale Date	Sale Website	Purchase Price	Sale Price	Profit

Total

Purchase & Sales Tracker

DATES FROM _____

Item	Purchase Date	Sale Date	Sale Website	Purchase Price	Sale Price	Profit

Total

Purchase & Sales Tracker

DATES FROM _____

Item	Purchase Date	Sale Date	Sale Website	Purchase Price	Sale Price	Profit

Total

Purchase & Sales Tracker

DATES FROM _____

Item	Purchase Date	Sale Date	Sale Website	Purchase Price	Sale Price	Profit

Total

Purchase & Sales Tracker

DATES FROM _____

Item	Purchase Date	Sale Date	Sale Website	Purchase Price	Sale Price	Profit

Total

Purchase & Sales Tracker

DATES FROM _____

Item	Purchase Date	Sale Date	Sale Website	Purchase Price	Sale Price	Profit

Total

Purchase & Sales Tracker

DATES FROM _____

Item	Purchase Date	Sale Date	Sale Website	Purchase Price	Sale Price	Profit

Total

Purchase & Sales Tracker

DATES FROM _____

Item	Purchase Date	Sale Date	Sale Website	Purchase Price	Sale Price	Profit

Total

Purchase & Sales Tracker

DATES FROM _____

Item	Purchase Date	Sale Date	Sale Website	Purchase Price	Sale Price	Profit

Total | | |

Purchase & Sales Tracker

DATES FROM _____

Item	Purchase Date	Sale Date	Sale Website	Purchase Price	Sale Price	Profit

Total

Purchase & Sales Tracker

DATES FROM _____

Item	Purchase Date	Sale Date	Sale Website	Purchase Price	Sale Price	Profit

Total

Purchase & Sales Tracker

DATES FROM _____

Item	Purchase Date	Sale Date	Sale Website	Purchase Price	Sale Price	Profit

Total

Purchase & Sales Tracker

DATES FROM _____

Item	Purchase Date	Sale Date	Sale Website	Purchase Price	Sale Price	Profit

Total | | |

Purchase & Sales Tracker

DATES FROM _____

Item	Purchase Date	Sale Date	Sale Website	Purchase Price	Sale Price	Profit

Total

Purchase & Sales Tracker

DATES FROM _____

Item	Purchase Date	Sale Date	Sale Website	Purchase Price	Sale Price	Profit

Total

Purchase & Sales Tracker

DATES FROM _____

Item	Purchase Date	Sale Date	Sale Website	Purchase Price	Sale Price	Profit

Total

Purchase & Sales Tracker

DATES FROM _____

Item	Purchase Date	Sale Date	Sale Website	Purchase Price	Sale Price	Profit

	Total			

Purchase & Sales Tracker

DATES FROM _____

Item	Purchase Date	Sale Date	Sale Website	Purchase Price	Sale Price	Profit

Total

Purchase & Sales Tracker

DATES FROM _____

Item	Purchase Date	Sale Date	Sale Website	Purchase Price	Sale Price	Profit

Total

Purchase & Sales Tracker

DATES FROM _____

Item	Purchase Date	Sale Date	Sale Website	Purchase Price	Sale Price	Profit

Total

Purchase & Sales Tracker

DATES FROM _____

Item	Purchase Date	Sale Date	Sale Website	Purchase Price	Sale Price	Profit

Total

Purchase & Sales Tracker

DATES FROM _____

Item	Purchase Date	Sale Date	Sale Website	Purchase Price	Sale Price	Profit

Total

Purchase & Sales Tracker

DATES FROM _____

Item	Purchase Date	Sale Date	Sale Website	Purchase Price	Sale Price	Profit

Total

Purchase & Sales Tracker

DATES FROM _____

Item	Purchase Date	Sale Date	Sale Website	Purchase Price	Sale Price	Profit

Total

Purchase & Sales Tracker

DATES FROM _____

Item	Purchase Date	Sale Date	Sale Website	Purchase Price	Sale Price	Profit

Total _____

Purchase & Sales Tracker

Item	Purchase Date	Sale Date	Sale Website	Purchase Price	Sale Price	Profit

Total

Purchase & Sales Tracker

DATES FROM _____

Item	Purchase Date	Sale Date	Sale Website	Purchase Price	Sale Price	Profit

Total

Purchase & Sales Tracker

DATES FROM _____

Item	Purchase Date	Sale Date	Sale Website	Purchase Price	Sale Price	Profit

Total

Purchase & Sales Tracker

DATES FROM _____

Item	Purchase Date	Sale Date	Sale Website	Purchase Price	Sale Price	Profit

Total | | |

Purchase & Sales Tracker

Item	Purchase Date	Sale Date	Sale Website	Purchase Price	Sale Price	Profit

Total

Purchase & Sales Tracker

DATES FROM _____

Item	Purchase Date	Sale Date	Sale Website	Purchase Price	Sale Price	Profit

Total

Purchase & Sales Tracker

DATES FROM _____

Item	Purchase Date	Sale Date	Sale Website	Purchase Price	Sale Price	Profit

Total

Purchase & Sales Tracker

DATES FROM _____

Item	Purchase Date	Sale Date	Sale Website	Purchase Price	Sale Price	Profit

Total

Purchase & Sales Tracker

DATES FROM _____

Item	Purchase Date	Sale Date	Sale Website	Purchase Price	Sale Price	Profit

Total

Purchase & Sales Tracker

DATES FROM _____

Item	Purchase Date	Sale Date	Sale Website	Purchase Price	Sale Price	Profit

Total

Purchase & Sales Tracker

DATES FROM _____

Item	Purchase Date	Sale Date	Sale Website	Purchase Price	Sale Price	Profit

Total

Purchase & Sales Tracker

DATES FROM _____

Item	Purchase Date	Sale Date	Sale Website	Purchase Price	Sale Price	Profit

Total

Purchase & Sales Tracker

DATES FROM _____

Item	Purchase Date	Sale Date	Sale Website	Purchase Price	Sale Price	Profit

Total

Purchase & Sales Tracker

DATES FROM _____

Item	Purchase Date	Sale Date	Sale Website	Purchase Price	Sale Price	Profit

Total

Purchase & Sales Tracker

DATES FROM _____

Item	Purchase Date	Sale Date	Sale Website	Purchase Price	Sale Price	Profit

Total

Purchase & Sales Tracker

DATES FROM _____

Item	Purchase Date	Sale Date	Sale Website	Purchase Price	Sale Price	Profit

Total

Purchase & Sales Tracker

DATES FROM _____

Item	Purchase Date	Sale Date	Sale Website	Purchase Price	Sale Price	Profit

Total [   ] [   ] [   ]

Purchase & Sales Tracker

DATES FROM _____

Item	Purchase Date	Sale Date	Sale Website	Purchase Price	Sale Price	Profit

Total

Purchase & Sales Tracker

DATES FROM _____

Item	Purchase Date	Sale Date	Sale Website	Purchase Price	Sale Price	Profit

Total

Purchase & Sales Tracker

DATES FROM _____

Item	Purchase Date	Sale Date	Sale Website	Purchase Price	Sale Price	Profit

Total | | | |

Purchase & Sales Tracker

DATES FROM _____

Item	Purchase Date	Sale Date	Sale Website	Purchase Price	Sale Price	Profit

Total

Purchase & Sales Tracker

DATES FROM _____

Item	Purchase Date	Sale Date	Sale Website	Purchase Price	Sale Price	Profit

Total

Purchase & Sales Tracker

Item	Purchase Date	Sale Date	Sale Website	Purchase Price	Sale Price	Profit

Total

Purchase & Sales Tracker

DATES FROM _____

Item	Purchase Date	Sale Date	Sale Website	Purchase Price	Sale Price	Profit

Total

Purchase & Sales Tracker

DATES FROM _____

Item	Purchase Date	Sale Date	Sale Website	Purchase Price	Sale Price	Profit

Total

Purchase & Sales Tracker

DATES FROM _____

Item	Purchase Date	Sale Date	Sale Website	Purchase Price	Sale Price	Profit

Total

Purchase & Sales Tracker

DATES FROM _____

Item	Purchase Date	Sale Date	Sale Website	Purchase Price	Sale Price	Profit

Total

Purchase & Sales Tracker

DATES FROM _____

Item	Purchase Date	Sale Date	Sale Website	Purchase Price	Sale Price	Profit

Total

Purchase & Sales Tracker

DATES FROM _____

Item	Purchase Date	Sale Date	Sale Website	Purchase Price	Sale Price	Profit

Total

Purchase & Sales Tracker

DATES FROM _____

Item	Purchase Date	Sale Date	Sale Website	Purchase Price	Sale Price	Profit

Total

Purchase & Sales Tracker

DATES FROM _____

Item	Purchase Date	Sale Date	Sale Website	Purchase Price	Sale Price	Profit

Total

Purchase & Sales Tracker

DATES FROM _____

Item	Purchase Date	Sale Date	Sale Website	Purchase Price	Sale Price	Profit

Total | | | |

Purchase & Sales Tracker

DATES FROM _____

Item	Purchase Date	Sale Date	Sale Website	Purchase Price	Sale Price	Profit

Total

Purchase & Sales Tracker

DATES FROM _____

Item	Purchase Date	Sale Date	Sale Website	Purchase Price	Sale Price	Profit

Total

Purchase & Sales Tracker

DATES FROM _____

Item	Purchase Date	Sale Date	Sale Website	Purchase Price	Sale Price	Profit

Total

Purchase & Sales Tracker

DATES FROM _____

Item	Purchase Date	Sale Date	Sale Website	Purchase Price	Sale Price	Profit

Total

Purchase & Sales Tracker

Item	Purchase Date	Sale Date	Sale Website	Purchase Price	Sale Price	Profit

Total

Purchase & Sales Tracker

DATES FROM _____

Item	Purchase Date	Sale Date	Sale Website	Purchase Price	Sale Price	Profit

Total | | | |

Purchase & Sales Tracker

DATES FROM _____

Item	Purchase Date	Sale Date	Sale Website	Purchase Price	Sale Price	Profit

Total

Purchase & Sales Tracker

DATES FROM _____

Item	Purchase Date	Sale Date	Sale Website	Purchase Price	Sale Price	Profit

Total

Purchase & Sales Tracker

DATES FROM _____

Item	Purchase Date	Sale Date	Sale Website	Purchase Price	Sale Price	Profit

Total

Purchase & Sales Tracker

DATES FROM _____

Item	Purchase Date	Sale Date	Sale Website	Purchase Price	Sale Price	Profit

Total

Purchase & Sales Tracker

DATES FROM _____

Item	Purchase Date	Sale Date	Sale Website	Purchase Price	Sale Price	Profit

Total

Purchase & Sales Tracker

DATES FROM _____

Item	Purchase Date	Sale Date	Sale Website	Purchase Price	Sale Price	Profit

Total

Purchase & Sales Tracker

DATES FROM _____

Item	Purchase Date	Sale Date	Sale Website	Purchase Price	Sale Price	Profit

Total

Purchase & Sales Tracker

DATES FROM _____

Item	Purchase Date	Sale Date	Sale Website	Purchase Price	Sale Price	Profit

Total | | | |

Purchase & Sales Tracker

DATES FROM _____

Item	Purchase Date	Sale Date	Sale Website	Purchase Price	Sale Price	Profit

Total _____

Purchase & Sales Tracker

DATES FROM _____

Item	Purchase Date	Sale Date	Sale Website	Purchase Price	Sale Price	Profit

Total

Purchase & Sales Tracker

DATES FROM _____

Item	Purchase Date	Sale Date	Sale Website	Purchase Price	Sale Price	Profit

Total

Purchase & Sales Tracker

DATES FROM _____

Item	Purchase Date	Sale Date	Sale Website	Purchase Price	Sale Price	Profit

Total

Purchase & Sales Tracker

DATES FROM _____

Item	Purchase Date	Sale Date	Sale Website	Purchase Price	Sale Price	Profit

Total

Purchase & Sales Tracker

DATES FROM _____

Item	Purchase Date	Sale Date	Sale Website	Purchase Price	Sale Price	Profit

Total

Purchase & Sales Tracker

DATES FROM _____

Item	Purchase Date	Sale Date	Sale Website	Purchase Price	Sale Price	Profit

Total

Purchase & Sales Tracker

DATES FROM _____

Item	Purchase Date	Sale Date	Sale Website	Purchase Price	Sale Price	Profit

Total

Purchase & Sales Tracker

DATES FROM _____

Item	Purchase Date	Sale Date	Sale Website	Purchase Price	Sale Price	Profit

Total

Purchase & Sales Tracker

DATES FROM _____

Item	Purchase Date	Sale Date	Sale Website	Purchase Price	Sale Price	Profit

Total

Purchase & Sales Tracker

DATES FROM _____

Item	Purchase Date	Sale Date	Sale Website	Purchase Price	Sale Price	Profit

Total

Purchase & Sales Tracker

DATES FROM _____

Item	Purchase Date	Sale Date	Sale Website	Purchase Price	Sale Price	Profit

Total | | | |

Purchase & Sales Tracker

DATES FROM _____

Item	Purchase Date	Sale Date	Sale Website	Purchase Price	Sale Price	Profit

Total

Purchase & Sales Tracker

DATES FROM _____

Item	Purchase Date	Sale Date	Sale Website	Purchase Price	Sale Price	Profit

Total